Famous Illustrated
Speeches & Documents

The Statue of Liberty
"The New Colossus"

Stuart A. Kallen

Illustrated by Kristen Copham

Published by Abdo & Daughters, 4940 Viking Drive, Suite 622, Edina, Minnesota 55435.

Library bound edition distributed by Rockbottom Books, Pentagon Tower, P.O. Box 36036, Minneapolis, Minnesota 55435.

Printed in the United States.

Interior Photo credits: Bettmann.

Edited by Julie Berg

Kallen, Stuart A., 1955-
    The Statue of Liberty, "The New Colossus" / Stuart A. Kallen.
        p.   cm. -- (Famous Illustrated Speeches)
    Includes glossary
    ISBN 1-56239-315-4
    1. Statue of Liberty (New York, N.Y.) -- Juvenile literature.
    2. New York (N.Y.) -- Buildings, structures, etc. -- juvenile literature.
    [1. Statue of Liberty (New York, N.Y.) 2. National monuments.
    3. Statues.]   I. Title.   II. Series.
    F128.64.L6K35   1994
    974.7'1--dc20   94-13309
                                       CIP
                                       AC

INTRODUCTION

For more than one hundred years, she has held her torch high above New York Harbor. For the millions passing under her firm gaze, she has come to mean hope, freedom, and justice. At one time she was the largest statue in the world. Today she is wrapped as one with the American dream. It's easy to forget that she was a gift from France. Who is this woman of liberty and enlightenment that guards America's eastern shore? What is her story?

On June 21, 1871, a steamship sailed into the busy port on the southern tip of Manhattan. Aboard the ship were hundreds of immigrants seeking a new home in America. One of the passengers was 37-year-old French sculptor Frédéric Auguste Bartholdi. Bartholdi came to New York City that day to follow his own dream—a dream of building a huge statue that would be paid for by the people of France and given to the people of the United States as a token of friendship.

France had helped the United States in its struggle for independence from England in 1776. But by the time Bartholdi visited New York, France was ruled by the iron hand of Emperor Napoleon III. Bartholdi wished for the kind of freedom in France that was given to Americans by the U.S. Constitution. On a five-month visit to the United States, Bartholdi crossed the country meeting many Americans. Everywhere he went, people supported the dream of the Statue of Liberty.

Bartholdi returned to France and began work on his vision. By 1875 he had completed a four-foot-tall clay model of the statue. Then he began to raise the $400,000 it would take to complete the work. That task took six years.

While money was being donated, Bartholdi and his workers began to hammer together the world's largest statue. It was slow, painstaking work. Each section was built of huge wooden frames, pounded together by master carpenters. To size each section properly, over 9,000 measurements had to be taken. The frames were then covered with plaster. Next, copper sheets were hammered onto the plaster. In the courtyard next to the studio, Gustave Eiffel erected the framework that would hold up the statue. Eiffel would later become famous as the man who built the Eiffel Tower in Paris, France.

By the summer of 1883, the statue towered 151 feet above Bartholdi's Paris neighborhood. Twenty years after his dream began, he had finished his monument. He called his work Liberty Enlightening the World.

The statue was presented to the American ambassador to France on July 4, 1884. Then it was taken down and shipped piece by piece to New York Harbor. But the Americans had not raised enough money to build a base where the statue could be erected. Fund raising began for the pedestal. One way money was raised was with a poetry contest. A woman named Emma Lazarus entered a poem, "The New Colossus." Years later, that poem would be inscribed on the pedestal of the statue. The pedestal was finally completed in August 1886.

On October 28, 1886, President Grover Cleveland and thousands of New Yorkers gathered to dedicate the statue. The flag of France was draped over Liberty's face. When it was lowered, bells rang, ships' horns blared, and thousands cheered. Liberty Enlightening the World took her place on the world's stage.

Not like the brazen giant of Greek fame, with conquering limbs
astride from land to land;

Emma Lazarus wrote "The New Colossus" in 1883. She died of cancer at the age of 38 in 1887. The poem would not be carved into Liberty's pedestal until 1903.

Lazarus called her poem "The New Colossus." The old colossus was an enormous statue of the Greek sun-god Helios. This statue was also known as the Colossus of Rhodes. That bronze statue was 117 feet tall. It was finished in 280 B.C. and destroyed in an earthquake in 224 B.C.

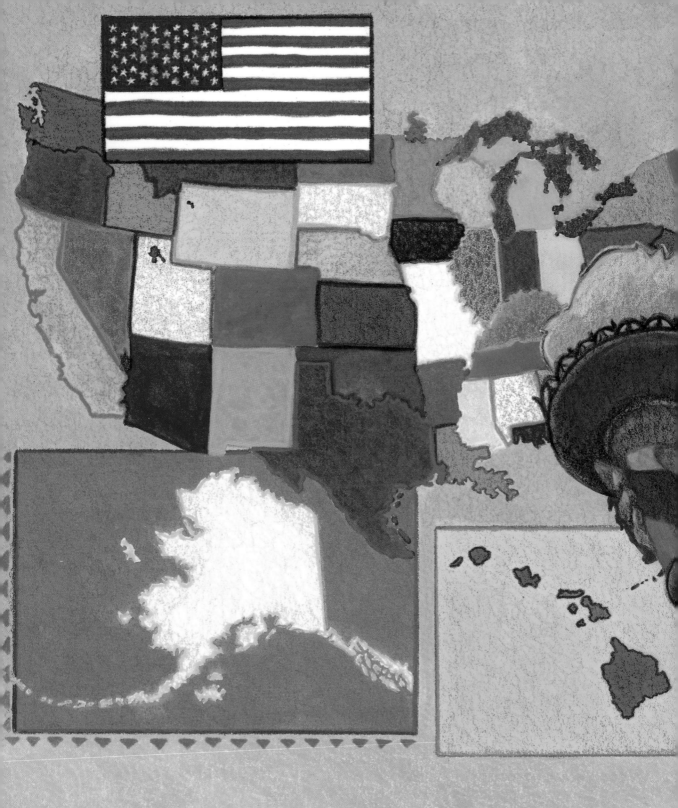

Here at our sea-washed, sunset gates shall stand a mighty woman with a torch,

The statue was mighty indeed. On her pedestal she stood 305 feet and 1 inch above the sea around her.

The giant Statue of Liberty is standing by the main entry port into the United States, holding her torch high.

whose flame is the imprisoned lightning

The first part of the statue to be completed was the right hand, the torch, and the flame. It amazed millions of people at the 1876 International Centennial Exhibition in Philadelphia.

The flame of freedom is more powerful than lightning.

and her name, Mother of Exiles.

When Lazarus wrote "The New Colossus" she was thinking of Jewish Russian refugees with whom she had worked. In Russia, many people were forced from their homes because of their beliefs.

Liberty was the mother of all people who left their own countries in search of freedom.

From her beacon-hand glows world-wide welcome;

When the Statue of Liberty was completed, people could climb a ladder, all the way up to the torch. This fine view of New York City was closed for safety reasons in 1916.

The light that liberty holds in her hand invites people from all over the world.

her mild eyes command the air-bridged harbor that twin cities frame.

The Brooklyn Bridge was more than one mile long and the towers that held it up were the largest man-made structure in America at the time.

When Lazarus wrote "The New Colossus" in 1883, the Brooklyn Bridge was near completion. It was an "air-bridge" across New York Harbor. The bridge joined the "twin cities" of Brooklyn and Manhattan which framed the harbor. Liberty's eyes ruled all.

"Keep ancient lands, your storied pomp!" cries she with silent lips.

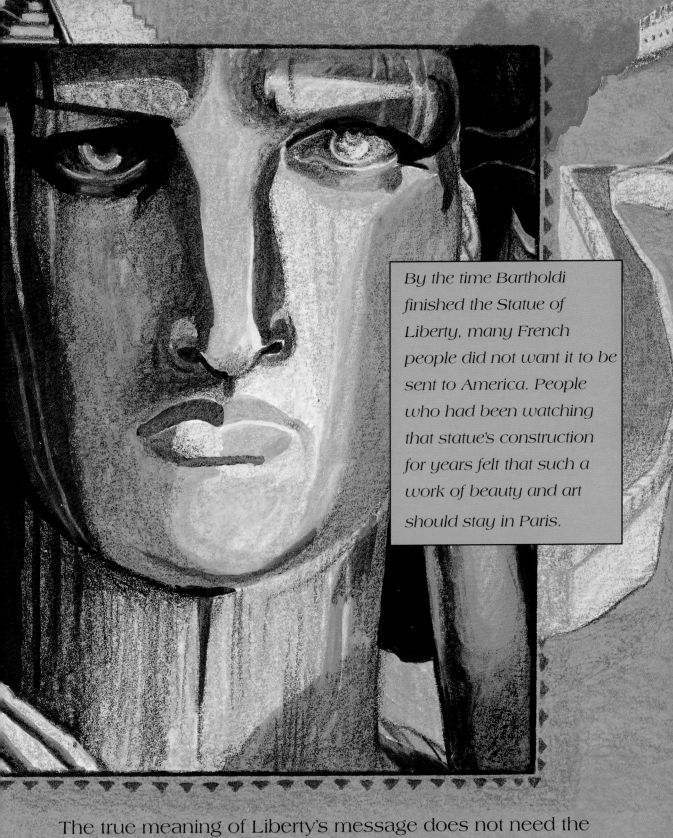

By the time Bartholdi finished the Statue of Liberty, many French people did not want it to be sent to America. People who had been watching that statue's construction for years felt that such a work of beauty and art should stay in Paris.

The true meaning of Liberty's message does not need the histories or customs of the Old World. "I don't need them," she cries through lips cast of copper.

"Give me your tired, your poor, your huddled masses.

Tens-of-millions of people moved to the United States from Europe in the century before Liberty's dedication. This was the largest mass movement of people in the history of the world.

The Statue of Liberty was offering a home to millions of tired and poor immigrants from other countries.

yearning to breathe free,

The journey to America took two or three months aboard dirty, crowded passenger ships. Robbery, seasickness, and starvation were common during passage.

The immigrants longed to be free. They traveled thousands of miles under harsh conditions to find political and religious freedom in the land of opportunity.

the wretched refuse of your teeming shore.

The flood of immigration before Liberty was built turned into a tidal wave afterwards. By 1925, 34 million people had moved from Europe to the United States.

Liberty was beckoning to people who were horribly unlucky and thought of as useless in their crowded homelands.

Send these, the homeless, tempest-tost to me,

Traveling took its toll in human life. One in ten passengers died aboard ship on their journey to the United States.

Liberty was welcoming the poor who were driven from their homes and shaken by the rough seas on the journey.

I lift my lamp beside the golden door!"

It is said today that the offspring of the men, women, and children who moved to the United States between 1880 and 1925 make up over half the U.S. population.

Liberty lifts her light of freedom next to the gateway of opportunity that was the United States.

The creators of the Statue of Liberty have long since passed away. Her shiny copper coat has turned a dull green. In 1904, Bartholdi became ill with tuberculosis. He cheerfully designed his own tombstone. When he was finished, he took to bed and died.

The only survivor of that era is Liberty herself. In 1916, a huge ammunition explosion on a nearby island caused her only slight damage. Even the light in her beacon did not flicker. Bartholdi said she would stand forever.

In 1903, Emma Lazarus' sonnet, "The New Colossus" was inscribed on a bronze plaque on Liberty's pedestal. In 1924, the statue and the island were named a national monument.

She has been called one of the great wonders of the world. The idea of freedom and liberty have come to represent what is best about the United States. With her steady gaze and her lamp held high, Liberty Enlightening the World guards those ideals for everyone.

THE NEW COLOSSUS - BY EMMA LAZARUS

Not like the brazen giant of Greek fame,

　　With conquering limbs astride from land to land;

　　Here at our sea-washed, sunset gates shall stand

A mighty woman with a torch, whose flame

Is the imprisoned lightning, and her name

　　Mother of Exiles. From her beacon-hand

　　Glows world-wide welcome; her mild eyes command

The air-bridged harbor that twin cities frame.

"Keep ancient lands, your storied pomp!" cries she

　　With silent lips. "Give me your tired, your poor,

Your huddled masses yearning to breathe free,

　　The wretched refuse of your teeming shore.

Send these, the homeless, tempest-tost to me,

　　I lift my lamp beside the golden door!"

GLOSSARY

Airbridge - suspended by cables.

Astride - with a leg on each side.

Beacon - a guiding light or signal.

Brazen - 1. something made of brass. 2. something bold.

Colossus - something gigantic and powerful.

Conquering - taking over by force.

Enlightenment - intellectual or spiritual knowledge.

Exile - separation from one's country or beliefs, usually by force.

Immigrant - a person who moves to another country for permanent residence.

Immigration - groups of people moving to another country for permanent residence.

Pedestal - a base for support of a statue.

Pomp - a vain display.

Refugee - a person who flees their homeland for safety or refuge in another country.

Refuse - anything thought of as worthless.

Restoration - to repair or bring back something that's old or damaged to a like-new state.

Sculptor - an artist who carves or models statues or art pieces out of stone, wood, clay, metal, etc.

Sonnet - a poem of 14 lines rhymed to a certain pattern.

Storied - celebrated in story or legend.

Teeming - to be overflowing or full.

Tempest - a sever storm with rain, hail, etc.

Wretched - horribly unfortunate or unlucky.

STATISTICS FOR THE STATUE OF LIBERTY

Height from base to torch - 305 ft., 1 in.

Height of statue - 151 ft., 1 in.

Length of torch - 21 ft.

Length of right arm - 42 ft.

Longest ray in crown - 11 ft., 6 in.

Length of head from chin to top - 17 ft., 3 in.

Head from ear to ear - 10 ft.

Distance across each eye - 2 ft., 6 in.

Length of nose - 4 ft., 6 in.

Width of mouth - 3 ft.

Index finger - 7 ft., 11 in.

Fingernail - 13 in. X 10 in.

Height of tablet - 23 ft., 7 in.

Thickness of waist - 35 ft.

Thickness of copper shell - 3/32 in.

Number of copper plates - 350

Steps in statue - 171

Weight of copper in statue - 100 tons or 200,000 pounds

Weight of skeleton - 125 tons or 250,000 pounds

Total weight of statue - 225 tons or 450,000 pounds